REPROGRAM YOUR MINDSET

100 Winning Quotes and Affirmations for High Performers

REPROGRAM YOUR MINDSET

100 Winning Quotes and Affirmations for High Performers

TONI A. HALEY, MD

REPROGRAM YOUR MINDSET
Published by Purposely Created Publishing Group™

Copyright © 2018 Toni Haley

All rights reserved.

No part of this book may be reproduced, distributed or transmitted in any form by any means, graphic, electronic, or mechanical, including photocopy, recording, taping, or by any information storage or retrieval system, without permission in writing from the publisher, except in the case of reprints in the context of reviews, quotes, or references.

Printed in the United States of America

ISBN: 978-1-948400-24-4

Special discounts are available on bulk quantity purchases by book clubs, associations and special interest groups. For details, email info@drtonimd.com or call 1-888-430-7431. For more information, log on to www.DrToniMD.com.

*"All the events you have experienced in
your lifetime up to this moment have
been created by your thoughts and beliefs
you have held in the past. They were created by the
thoughts and words
you used yesterday, last week,
last month, last year, 10, 20, 30, 40,
or more years ago, depending on
how old you are."*

Louise Hay, international bestselling author of
You Can Heal Your Life and a pioneer of the
self-empowerment movement
(1926–2017)

To my husband Reese,

Thank you for your love, faith, and support.

Thank you for preparing all my meals and prioritizing our goals.

I pray that I absorb your patience through osmosis.

I was "Winning" before we met, and now I have the "championship" ring.

You are the real MVP!

To my parents,

Thank you for loving me enough to ban excuses, whining, mediocrity or negative self-talk
in our home.

I am grateful for Family Meetings where I could assert myself and challenge the status quo.

You instilled resilience with tough love and a sprinkle of OCD.

As it turns out, this is a Winning combination.

You are my best coaches!

DOWNLOAD YOUR GIFTS!
FREE AUDIO COURSE

Thank you for purchasing my book!

To maximize your results, download the
FREE Master Your Mindset Master Class

DOWNLOAD YOUR GIFTS AT:
www.ReprogramYourMindset.com/gifts

Table of Contents

Gratitude xv
Foreword by Dr. Draion Burch xvii
Introduction 1

1. Affirmations 11
2. Early Career 13
3. The Boards and Other Big Tests 15
4. Spouses/Partners 17
5. Family 19
6. Friends 21
7. Happiness 23
8. Forgiveness 25
9. Procrastination 27
10. Health 29
11. Burnout 31
12. Success 33
13. Self-Love 35
14. Associates 37
15. Money 39
16. Negotiating 41
17. Communication 43
18. Public Speaking 45
19. Saying Yes to You 47
20. Pity Party 49
21. Perfectionism 51
22. Negative Thoughts 53
23. Negative Talk 55

24.	Settling	57
25.	Toxic Relationships	59
26.	Rejection	61
27.	Delayed Gratification	63
28.	Your Gifts	65
29.	Travel	67
30.	Habits	69
31.	Beauty	71
32.	Emotional Eating and Substance Use	73
33.	Obstacles	75
34.	Determination	77
35.	Expectations	79
36.	Parenthood	81
37.	Take Control	83
38.	Be the Change You Seek	85
39.	Passion	87
40.	Dreams	89
41.	Failure	91
42.	Setbacks	93
43.	Imposter Syndrome	95
44.	Choices	97
45.	Preparation	99
46.	Mistakes	101
47.	Freedom	103
48.	Dating	105
49.	Discrimination	107
50.	Vision and Affirmations	109
51.	Sexism	111
52.	#MeToo	113

53.	Patience	115
54.	Entrepreneurship	117
55.	Giving Back	119
56.	Stress	121
57.	Sleep	123
58.	Boundaries	125
59.	Self-Esteem	127
60.	Legacy	129
61.	Loneliness	131
62.	Faith	133
63.	Mental Health	135
64.	Losing	137
65.	Worry	139
66.	Love	141
67.	Death and Letting Go	143
68.	Vulnerability	145
69.	Comparison	147
70.	Debt	149
71.	Mentorship	151
72.	Networking	153
73.	Intuition	155
74.	Excuses	157
75.	Fancy Titles	159
76.	Awe	161
77.	Meditation	163
78.	Sponsorship	165
79.	Job Fit	167
80.	Criticism	169
81.	Regret	171

- 82. Motivation 173
- 83. Rules 175
- 84. Decisions 179
- 85. Guilt 181
- 86. Authenticity 181
- 87. Effort 183
- 88. Resilience 185
- 89. Work–Life Integration 187
- 90. Gratitude 189
- 91. Delegate and Reclaim Your Time ... 191
- 92. Live in the Moment 193
- 93. Leader versus Manager 195
- 94. Lifelong Learning 197
- 95. Motivating Others 199
- 96. Conflict 201
- 97. Micromanaging 203
- 98. Try Until You Win 205
- 99. Character 207
- 100. Best-Laid Plans 209

Final Thoughts 211

About the Author 215

Gratitude

Thank you for your support during this process.

This book was made possible due to the support and encouragement of several people.

Reese C. Haley
Tammy D. Jackson
Beverly L. Weston
Frank Williams, Jr.
Dr. Draion Burch
Pamela J. King
James Peyton
Dr. Tommie T. Easley
Leslie V. Horne
Sylvester Wynn Jones
Dr. Medell Briggs-Malonson
Dr. Shani K. Smith
Blaire Cann, Esq.

Foreword

Dear Readers,

Are you a high performer who is burned out? Are you a high performer who is overwhelmed at your J-O-B? Are you a high performer who prioritizes everyone and everything - BUT YOU? Are you a high performer who can't understand why you aren't "WINNING" at life? You are supposed to have it all, right? Or so, you thought. If you answered YES to ANY of these questions, this book written by Dr. Toni A. Haley is just for you. In this book, Dr. Toni teaches you how YOU CAN HAVE IT ALL!

Close your eyes and imagine what it will feel like to have everything you desire. Really picture what it will feel like to reach your "TRUE" goals. No, not the goals you tell your friends - the real goals - the ones you feel in your soul. You will have actionable steps to SAY YES to yourself and go after everything you want in life once you finish reading this book.

Let me introduce myself. I'm Dr. Drai, board-certified OBGYN, three-time bestselling author, international six-figure speaker, award-winning business coach, and Dean of an online Business School for medical professionals. I help doctors monetize their medical degree so they can walk in their purpose, create more profit, have the time, and freedom they deserve. I was so honored when Dr. Toni A. Haley asked me to write her foreword.

I met Dr. Toni in December 2016 during one of my online business trainings for doctors. I taught the students about "Planning for Profit" the night Dr. Toni showed up in my virtual classroom and immediately I knew she was a winner. When other students would sabotage themselves during Q & A, Dr. Toni would instantly help them re-structure their language. Ah Ha… Right before my eyes, I saw a doctor who was able to get other high performers to "WIN" when she changed their negative thoughts about themselves. A mindset master coach was born on that night. "Mental Attitude," having a positive mindset, is the core of Dr. Toni's WINNING formula. Write that down. I have coached hundreds of doctors and high performers so I know when a student has the gift of transformation. Dr. Toni has it and she's ready to change the world.

In January 2017, Dr. Toni set up an appointment with me to discuss how we could work together. I remember that conversation: "Dr. Drai, I want to get in the school now. I'm over-ready to help high performers reach the life they envisioned before graduate school." Our school was completely full at that time. But…when the pupil is ready, the teacher appears. I knew she could transform lives because I witnessed it during the online trainings. So, we got to work and spent ten months together building her legacy. Here's the key to Dr. Toni's success. Get out a pen & paper to write these four things down:

1. She always takes imperfect action.
2. She does not self-sabotage.
3. She has a positive mindset.
4. She has a supportive partner (her husband, Reese) who also wants her to win.

Dr. Toni has already transformed several high performers' lives. And there are many more, just like you, waiting. In this book, Dr. Toni gives you a fail-proof system and the tools you need to take your life back - as long as you do the work. Read it more than once. Buy a copy for your friends or colleagues who also may need help "WINNING." Dr. Toni, thank you for sharing your GIFT with the world. I'm so proud of you.

Dr. Drai
Dean of Medical Moguls Academy

Introduction

Are you wondering how you made it this far in life and still feel stuck? Are you wondering why you are still not "Winning" big after so many years of sacrifice, working holidays and missing family gatherings? Are you overwhelmed, struggling with failure or not satisfied with how you spend your limited free time? What happened after the initial excitement when the graduate school admission letter news faded? When you walked across the stage at the top of your class with accolades and honors, with all the fanfare, robes, and tassels - you thought it was over, right? You finally got the "dream job," but it wasn't quite what you wanted? Do you feel like a fraud sometimes and hope no one finds out how much you worry about being *perfect*? Winners, raise your hand if you can relate to any of these situations. I know how it feels to be stuck and it is time you changed your mind to free yourself. It is time for you to break out of the box and Win BIGGER!

So who am I and how can I help you? I am Dr. Toni A. Haley, a board-certified family medicine physician, wife, and coach. I help high performers, like myself, take control of their careers, love life, and lifestyle. Many of us high performers are burned out and are tired of being taken for granted. You may not know where to begin, but are considering a change for the better. Many of my clients relate to my story of empowerment after failure and burnout led me to a wake-up call. It was not that long ago that I was on the verge of a failed career, failed marriage, filed bankruptcy and was dangerously overweight.

I remember the beginning very clearly. It started one gloomy, overcast day in Pittsburgh when I was about eight years old. The test results were in. I set the table for dinner like I always did. I stood on my step stool and took extra long with the salad spinner, watching the lettuce whiz by and hoping time would too because we were having a family meeting after dinner. These meetings were only fun if you decided the topic of discussion, so I was dreading it. The good news was - we were having my favorite: oven-fried chicken wings with salad and Rice-A-Roni. The bad news was - I feared the test results would be disappointing. I chewed every bite about a hundred times but I barely tasted anything. My life was forever altered that day…all because of an IQ test. My life became a whirlwind of activities and schedules after the test results. The Center for Advanced Studies suddenly became the epicenter of my universe.

I was placed in an elite class with other bright youngsters. By the time I was in middle school, I was in Student Council, played violin in the City Youth Orchestra, studied Tae Kwon Do, and took architecture courses in addition to my core science and mathematics curriculum. Back then, magnet schools were all the rage to prepare for a career in STEM (science, technology, engineering, and mathematics). High school was even more challenging. I added college prep courses, cheerleading, marching band, and college chemistry at the University of Pittsburgh while I also held an office for the weekly Medical Explorers club at the medical school. You name it, I was involved. I was learning hands-on at the morgue from the coroner and was fascinated by the buckets of organs. Open-heart surgery after SAT prep before theater class? Sure, sign me up!

Now, you have to ask yourself, what makes a high performer? For me, being a high performer and an overachiever was my passport to freedom. My life changed in an instant when I was three years old. My father was in his early twenties at the time and received a call that his wife and daughter were in a motor vehicle accident. He raced to the hospital to collect us. When he arrived, he was informed I was the sole survivor of the accident. It was then that Daddy became overprotective. I had to have a real good reason to leave the house. Frankly, a permission slip was usually required. So all of my activities allowed me to embrace the world on my terms and strive for an exit to my future.

The effort paid off when I was awarded over $150,000 in academic scholarships to attend college out of state. I was on my way to pursue my dream of becoming a doctor! I kept up the same pace in college throughout the academic year and signed up for summer programs.

I was busy and focused but I never really assessed my own needs or found a good balance. I started looking for a way to take a break after becoming burned out. When I received the call that my grandmother was fighting lung cancer, it was the perfect solution. I collected my honors diploma and returned home to assist my family with my grandmother's care. After her death, the reality of my restrictive home environment led to depression. I no longer recognized myself in the mirror. Gone was the cheerleader with a word of encouragement for someone else. It was hard to give myself a pep talk, let alone find the energy to get back on track. It was during this time and my quest for freedom and independence that my first husband found me.

He showed up ready to teach me to drive at twenty-four years old! He bought my first car as an engagement present. Looking back, it was pretty liberating but three years into the marriage I realized we wanted different things for the future. I knew I had to return to the pursuit of medicine if I was to be financially sound on my own. My first husband helped me rediscover my initial ambition to become a physician. It was time for me to get back in the game and off the sidelines. I was accepted into medical school but not without a major shift in lifestyle. Struggling to study, pay for school, and pay for the divorce caused me to gain weight and lose confidence. I began grieving the loss of the life I had envisioned. My licensing exams were on the line and my professors began to question my commitment. Even I did not recognize myself. I was miserable, obese, and in danger of failing out of medical school because my focus was not on passing the Medical Board Exams. I knew I had to make a change and salvage my dreams.

For the first time in my life, I gave myself permission to take care of me. I put my needs first. When you are up against the wall, you have to work on your mindset. You have to shift your thoughts and your focus. I cancelled the pity party and committed to being an example for my patients and colleagues. I confronted the negative thoughts, worked on my low self-esteem and identified what I wanted. I wanted to be a doctor. I wanted a husband to share the journey and to feel whole as a woman. I had a clear vision of walking across the stage at my residency graduation with my husband waiting for me on the other side. I was told I was crazy to date while in post-graduate training. I was told to lower my standards. But the naysayers did not deter me. I recovered from failure, met my current husband, Reese, and completed residency with him at my side. As a result of embracing change, I am living the dreams I had when I was ten years old. Now, I work closely with high performers and achievers in my coaching programs to maximize their personal and professional potential so they can get out their own heads and Win in every area of their lives!

If you wonder how other Winners are thriving when

you are barely making it through the day or week, this book is exactly what the doctor ordered! You followed all the rules, listened to your family and mentors but are still not where you imagined. If you are ready to stop feeling sorry for yourself and reclaim your power and focus, keep reading. If you deserve better but struggle to speak up, you are going to find this book helpful. This is a "playbook" to help you reframe your thoughts to get closer to the life you deserve and that you earned. You will be inspired by the sage wisdom and quotes from other successful leaders. Learning to frame your thoughts with personalized affirmations and will affirm your potential and reprogram your mind to win!

Write and practice saying your personalized affirmations aloud daily.

Why you need affirmations

> *"When you enter a mindset, you enter a new world. In one world--the world of fixed traits—success is about proving you're smart or talented. In the other—the world of changing qualities—it's about stretching yourself to learn something new...Mindsets are just beliefs. They're powerful beliefs, but they're just something in your mind, and you can change your mind."*
>
> *~ Carol Dweck, PhD, world-renowned Stanford University psychologist and leading authority on Mindset.*

Remember that first big win? You filled out hundreds of applications and interviewed so much you were tired of wearing the suit! Finally, you got it! You were so excited to call everyone to tell them that you got into the top program or were promoted. But the fun didn't last. You became keenly aware that this was a lot of work and you started forgetting how illustrious the position was and how happy you were when it was offered. You started to stress and worry. You became more overwhelmed and less grateful.

What if you start each day with a positive routine that included words and thoughts to quiet the negative voice in your head? Starting each day with affirmations and reminders of how blessed you are will keep you on track. What you focus on will intensify and multiply. It is important that your mind is centered only on greatness to attract and keep the good flowing in your life! Once I made affirmations a priority, those depressing thoughts fell away. I knew I was not a failure just because things did not go as planned. All your hopes and desires take shape and you start to attract good things.

Affirmations keep things in perspective and allow you to constantly course correct.

How to Win with affirmations

1. Write affirmations in the first person. Use "I" statements.
2. Use "I am" as a declaration to help you get used to the idea.

3. Use *action* verbs to bring energy to your words and thoughts.
4. Only speak in the present tense, as if it is already your reality.
5. Repeat affirmations daily—preferably every morning, afternoon and night.
6. Select your favorite personalized affirmations and post them where you can see them each day. Put them on the bathroom mirror, bathroom wall, nightstand, refrigerator, phone or computer screensaver, closet door, desk calendar or ceiling above the bed!
7. Visualize your life. Picture how it will look, feel, smell and revisit these images every day as you fall asleep, while repeating your personalized affirmations.
8. Take ACTION. To help you with this process, I have provided a space after each section in this book, so you can reflect and write notes in the lines provided. For each section, think about the following questions as it pertains to the corresponding subject:
    1. What steps will you take to start NOW?
    2. How will you make this a habit?
    3. Who will hold you accountable?

Once I saw the value of affirmations, I made up my mind to change the narrative of doubt, worry and fear playing on "repeat" in my mind. Everything improved and insomnia faded away. I am a living, breathing testament to the fact that you can indeed design your ideal life, no matter the setback or obstacle. As a high performer, you already know you have to work to get results. Use the quotes to help you focus on generating what you want and articulating your personal affirmations. Remember, the life you envision starts with what you tell yourself every single day.

1. Affirmations

"Affirmation without discipline is the beginning of delusion."

- Jim Rohn, entrepreneur, author and motivational speaker

Did you *really* think you were going to speak your affirmations, without following through with your plan and action steps? No dreams are fulfilled without good old-fashioned sweat equity. A childhood mentor once told me, "God expects us to put legs on our prayers."

Example Affirmation: I take action on my affirmations.

Personalized Affirmation:

_____

_____

_____

_____

_____

_____

2. Early Career

"I hated every minute of the training, but I said: 'Don't quit. Suffer now and live the rest of your life as a champion.'"

- Muhammad Ali, boxing legend and sports icon

Congratulations! You made it! You are on your way to the career you dreamed of for years! Many worry, "Am I good enough?" Are you concerned they won't think you are qualified? Are you looking around for someone who's more qualified? Guess what? You are it, and you are ready.

Example Affirmation: I am enough. I am qualified. I am ready to WIN!

Personalized Affirmation:

_____

_____

_____

_____

_____

Toni A. Haley, MD

3. The Boards and Other Big Tests

"If my future were determined just by my performance on a standardized test, I wouldn't be here. I guarantee you that."

- Michelle Obama, former First Lady of the United States

At some point, you have fretted over standardized tests or medical specialty boards. There are many "tests" to become a doctor and even more as you ascend in your career. Sometimes, "the test" is deciding which job or work setting is right for you. Choosing a seemingly lucrative opportunity versus one that just feels right in your heart. Thankfully, none of these tests define you. Make the best decision you can and move forward.

Example Affirmation: I am choosing wisely when facing any test.

Personalized Affirmation:

_____

_____

_____

4. Spouses/Partners

"...your marriage doesn't start when you say 'I do,' your marriage starts when you look over at your partner and you want to kill 'em...and then the next minute you say I love them more than anything and I'm sticking [to] it."

-Viola Davis, the first black woman to win an Oscar, Emmy and Tony Award for acting

After being married twice, I can attest to the need for effective communication with your spouse or partner. You are on the same team and can push each other's buttons, but once you commit, remain open-minded. Acknowledge their perspective because the *mutual love and respect* will carry you through many challenges.

Example Affirmation: I am committed to effective communication and teamwork.

Personalized Affirmation:

_____

_____

_____

_____

5. Family

"My mom has made it possible for me to be who I am. Our family is everything. Her greatest skill was encouraging me to find my own person and own independence."

- Charlize Theron, actress

Your family loves you, but if yours is anything like mine, they do not always know what is right for you. Everyone has an opinion or is a critic. Especially family. Winners do not allow others to project external fears or worry into their decision-making.

Example: My family accepts and loves me even if my approach is different.

Personalized Affirmation:

_____

_____

_____

_____

_____

_____

6. Friends

"Lots of people want to ride with you in the limo, but what you want is someone who will take the bus with you when the limo breaks down."

- **Oprah Winfrey, media icon and philanthropist**

Your friendships are tested during the arduous journey of graduate school, medical training, working and building a business. Cherish those who earned the privilege of being in your inner circle. Winners seek people who bring out their best qualities and avoid those who are jealous or negative. Choose wisely.

Example Affirmation: I am worthy of loyal, supportive, fulfilling friendships.

Personalized Affirmation:

_____

_____

_____

_____

_____

1. Happiness

Happiness is "the experience of joy, contentment, or positive well-being, combined with a sense that one's life is good, meaningful, and worthwhile."

> \- Sonja Lyubomirsky, PhD and author of
> *The How of Happiness*

Do you want to be happier? Winners can control their perspective and evoke *happy* feelings at will. You can appreciate your life right now and draw others closer. Winners attract the positive and enhance their mood by helping others and spreading the love!

Example: I deserve happiness and can control my emotions.

Personalized Affirmation:

_____

_____

_____

_____

_____

8. Forgiveness

"The weak can never forgive. Forgiveness is the attribute of the strong."

　　　　　–Mahatma Gandhi, activist and leader

Let go of the pain, disappointment or perceived slight. Give yourself some grace and forgive yourself for bad choices. Power is in forgiveness and in moving forward. Winners, forgiveness is for you, not the person that hurt you or let you down.

Example: I am forgiving myself and others while releasing negative emotions.

Personalized Affirmation:

_____

_____

_____

_____

_____

_____

9. Procrastination

"If you spend too much time thinking about a thing, you'll never get it done."

- Bruce Lee, martial artist and cultural icon

When you looked at your calendar there was so much time. Now, you are pressed to get it done and are up against the wall. Prioritize your most urgent, complex tasks. Eliminate all distractions and no interruptions until your top priorities are complete.

Example Affirmation: I am completing complicated tasks FIRST without interruption.

Personalized Affirmation:

_____

_____

_____

_____

_____

_____

10. Health

"Health is not valued till sickness comes."
– Dr. Thomas Fuller, 17th-century scholar, preacher and author

---

Value your health so you can serve and live out your mission. Even physicians know better, but still have higher rates of substance abuse, suicide and motor vehicle accidents than the general population, according to a 2014 Mayo Clinic study. Model good health for your loved ones because prevention is the best medicine.

Example Affirmation: I am inspiring others by making healthy choices.

Personalized Affirmation:

_____

_____

_____

_____

_____

_____

11. Burnout

"Some people don't like change, but you need to embrace change if the alternative is disaster."

- Elon Musk, billionaire, engineer, CEO and co-founder of Tesla.

Burnout does not make you weak, but it is common in high performers. Over 50 percent of physicians are experiencing at least one symptom of burnout in the United States and has been declared a national public health crisis! Many successful people in stressful jobs report depression, have suicidal thoughts, emotional exhaustion, cynicism or a reduced sense of accomplishment. Seek help if you are experiencing signs of depression or burnout.

Example Affirmation: My mental and physical health is a top priority.

Personalized Affirmation:

_____

_____

_____

12. Success

"Warren Buffett has always said the measure [of success] is whether the people close to you are happy and love you."

   - **Bill Gates, Business Magnate and Philanthropist.**

Strive for a sense of well-being and fulfillment. Billionaires Oprah Winfrey, Bill Gates and Sir Richard Branson believe success is about making an impact on society and leaving a legacy. How do you measure success beyond money, titles, and power?

Example Affirmation: I am successful when I seek joy, fulfillment and quality time.

Personalized Affirmation:

_____

_____

_____

_____

_____

_____

13. Self-Love

"I believe that the greatest gift you can give your family and the world is a healthy you."

- Joyce Meyer, Bible teacher and survivor of incest, emotional and physical abuse

You are worthy of love and a healthy self-image, no matter what happened in the past. When you love yourself, you will find courage and power to speak up. *You will not allow others to take you for granted, diminish your achievements or mistreat you.* Nurture yourself with planned "mental health days" where you have quiet time alone and no one knows you are on vacation. Sleep, exercise, take a long bath, enjoy regular massage therapy or spa retreats. The anxiety and need to please others will fade, and peace will emerge.

Example Affirmation: I am loving myself first because I am deserving.

Personalized Affirmation:

_____

_____

Toni A. Haley, MD

14. Associates

"You will move in the direction of the people that you associate with…it's important to associate with people that are better than yourself."

- Warren Buffett, business magnate and philanthropist

Be careful not to become complacent and work in a silo. Seek out those who are growing, learning and will challenge you to do the same. If you are the smartest person in the room, find a better room. The trajectory of your career and success may depend largely on your ability to connect with associates and network.

Example Affirmation: I am connecting with dynamic colleagues who challenge me to grow.

Personalized Affirmation:

_____

_____

_____

_____

15. Money

"Do good, have fun and the money will come."

— **Sir Richard Branson, business mogul and philanthropist**

How you feel about yourself is directly correlated to how much money you will make! Just as you deserve to be happy, you deserve wealth and abundance. If you do not have enough money, you can align your heart, mind and energy to change that right now!

Example Affirmation: I am a money-making doctor!

Personalized Affirmation:

_____

_____

_____

_____

_____

_____

_____

16. Negotiating

"Let us never negotiate out of fear. But let us never fear to negotiate."

- John F. Kennedy, former president of the United States

Winners know you do not get what you deserve. You get what you negotiate! Only sit down to the proverbial table with those who have the power to make a decision and possess similar values, goals and interests. Come ready with your signature style, personality and big sexy brain. Closed mouths don't get fed, so speak up for yourself. *The best negotiations are a win–win for all parties.*

Example Affirmation: I am confident, prepared and committed to a Win-Win negotiation.

Personalized Affirmation:

_____

_____

_____

_____

Toni A. Haley, MD

17. Communication

"Your ability to communicate is an important tool in pursuit of your goals, whether it is with your family, your coworkers or your clients and customers."

- **Les Brown, motivational speaker and author**

Focus on listening and communicating clearly with patients to improve clinical outcomes. It also can increase your job satisfaction, thereby reducing stress and burnout.

Example Affirmation: I am capable of improving relationships with better listening, questions and communication.

Personalized Affirmation:

_____

_____

_____

_____

_____

_____

18. Public Speaking

"I used to stutter really badly. Everybody thinks it's funny. And it's not funny. It's not."

- **Joe Biden, former vice president of the United States**

Don't let fear, embarrassment or anxiety keep you from the highest office in the land. You are smart and you are a very big deal! People will pay to hear what you have to say once you prepare properly. Join a speaking club or hire a coach to practice and get constructive feedback. Skip the boring slide presentations. Choose a topic that you are passionate about and share your story and expertise!

Example Affirmation: I am worthy to speak on any stage.

Personalized Affirmation:

_____

_____

_____

_____

19. Saying Yes to You

"Losing yourself does not happen all at once. Losing yourself happens one NO at a time."

- Shonda Rhimes, TV producer and author

Tired of being unappreciated? Do you want less frustration and resentment? Stop talking yourself out of the things that nurture you. Say YES to yourself. The positive side effect may be a sense of well-being, self-worth and less stress. You may notice things that matter to you may actually get done when you put yourself first. How often do you say NO to things that do not honor your values?

Example Affirmation: I am saying yes to my happiness, joy and reclaiming balance in my life. I confidently say yes to me.

Personalized Affirmation:

_____

_____

_____

_____

20. Pity Party

"I have not failed. I've just found 10,000 ways that won't work."

- Thomas Edison, inventor

Do you think you were the first to be embarrassed, to be frustrated, or to want to quit? You did not invent failure and you will not be the last to experience disappointment. Limit the pity party, learn from the fall, and move on quickly. Your triumph will erase all the hurt and exhaustion.

Example Affirmation: As long as I am moving forward and learning, I am Winning.

Personalized Affirmation:

_____

_____

_____

_____

_____

21. Perfectionism

"I am careful not to confuse excellence with perfection. Excellence I can reach for; perfection is God's business."

- Michael J. Fox, actor and activist

Winners always aim high. Unfortunately, when you focus on getting the details perfect, you may lose joy on the journey. Do the best you can with what you have and take action. No one will ever know how good you are if you hesitate at every turn.

Example Affirmation: I am taking steps forward despite imperfections.

Personalized Affirmation:

_____

_____

_____

_____

_____

_____

22. Negative Thoughts

"I don't have the best self-esteem; mine wavers month to month, but I know how to pick myself up."

- **Tyra Banks, creator of America's Next Top Model, actress and business woman**

Ruminating on where you fall short or focusing on being perfect leaves little room for a positive outlook. Write down all of your negative thoughts and emotions, then ceremoniously burn them or throw them in the trash. Challenge yourself by asking, "Is this true, or am I being too hard on myself?" Write a positive list of your attributes to counteract the negative thoughts running through your head.

Example Affirmation: I control the narrative in my mind and choose positive thoughts.

Personalized Affirmation:

_____

_____

_____

_____

23. Negative Talk

"Evidence is conclusive that your self-talk has a direct bearing on your performance."

- Zig Ziglar, motivational speaker and author

Be your own biggest fan! There are enough people with negative things to say. Ask yourself, "Am I being my own worst critic? Am I being too harsh?" Challenge that nagging, critical voice so when others attempt to speak negative words, it will not ring true. Give yourself the same encouragement and comforting words you would shower on your loved ones.

Example Affirmation: I will take positive action and speak positive words.

Personalized Affirmation:

_____

_____

_____

_____

24. Settling

"What we can or cannot do, what we consider possible or impossible, is rarely a function of our true capability. It is more likely a function of our beliefs about who we are."

- **Tony Robbins, life and business strategist, philanthropist and author**

Set your sights beyond what you currently believe or can fathom. I employed this approach to find the husband of my dreams and to rebound after failure. Enhance your strengths to grow each day. Implement what you learn and take a leap of faith. *Achieve, reach higher, repeat.*

Example Affirmation: I am capable of better and I will not settle.

Personalized Affirmation:

_____

_____

_____

_____

_____

25. Toxic Relationships

"Negative people deplete your energy. Surround yourself with the love and nourishment and do not allow the creation of negativity in your environment."

–Deepak Chopra, author and alternative medicine advocate

Do you know anyone who is cynical and sucks all the joy out of the room? What about the people who turn every conversation to themselves? Some people have no respect for boundaries and ignore social graces. Avoid these types of people like you would avoid arsenic, carbon monoxide or lead exposure.

Example Affirmation: I am avoiding toxic people and relationships.

Personalized Affirmation:

_____

_____

_____

_____

26. Rejection

"I was told everyday I'd never be nothing. Now I look in the mirror and say, Tiffany Haddish, I love and approve of you, and it was all worth it...If I could make them laugh, I was less likely to get beat."

- Tiffany Haddish, comedian, actress and former foster child.

If folks are giving you the side eye or a bit of resistance, you are probably doing something to get noticed! When others reject you, push you away or treat you poorly, it may correlate to *their* insecurities or pain. That behavior denotes unresolved issues, and your reaction is how they gauge whether you are an easy target for more bullying or harassment. Know your value and remain stoic in the face of antagonism or ruffians.

Example Affirmation: I am free from fear of rejection

Personalized Affirmation:

_____

_____

_____

27. Delayed Gratification

"It always seems impossible until it's done."
- **Nelson Mandela, political leader and philanthropist**

As much as you want to walk away when the going gets tough, *stay the course*. You knew quitting college or graduate school was not an option. What can you do with partial credit towards an advanced degree? The sacrifice will pay off when you devise the best plan to utilize your strengths.

Example Affirmation: I am committed to long-term benefits of my sacrifice today.

Personalized Affirmation:

_____

_____

_____

_____

_____

_____

28. Your Gifts

"I have no special talent. I am only passionately curious."
       - **Albert Einstein, theoretical physicist**

Day one of anatomy and physiology, it was likely overwhelming to learn all 206 bones in the human body. Looking back, you got through some milestones on passion and enthusiasm alone! Once you have finally mastered the basics, create based on your unique gifts or talents! Don't allow ideas to lie dormant in the back of your mind.

Example Affirmation: I am passionate about discovering my unique gifts.

Personalized Affirmation:

_____

_____

_____

_____

_____

29. Travel

"Though we travel the world over to find the beautiful, we must carry it with us or we find it not."

- Ralph Waldo Emerson, philosopher and poet

Winners who explore build confidence and tap into their creativity. Travel is liberating, stress relieving and is good for your overall well-being. Travel enhances empathy and improves your world view, which you carry everywhere you go.

Example Affirmation: I will travel to elevate my mind.

Personalized Affirmation:

_____

_____

_____

_____

_____

_____

_____

30. Habits

"We are what we repeatedly do. Excellence, then, is not an act, but a habit."

- Aristotle, Greek philosopher

New Year's resolutions are often abandoned after a few days, weeks, or months. Eliminate bad habits and toxic relationships to Win big *daily*. Focus on your nutrition, get enough sleep, exercise, and drink your water. You are so good at telling others what to do, please take your own advice because health is often determined by your daily habits.

Example Affirmation: I am Winning by practicing good habits every day.

Personalized Affirmation:

_____

_____

_____

_____

_____

31. Beauty

"I hope that my presence on your screen and my face in magazines may lead you young girls on a beautiful journey that you will feel validation of your external beauty, but also get to the deeper business of being beautiful inside."

- Lupita Nyong'o, actress and Academy Award winner

Winners possess inner beauty that reflects on the outside. When the makeup, Spanx and photo filters are removed, your radiance should still shine brightly. How you feel about yourself correlates with confidence and wealth.

Example Affirmation: I am enhancing my inner beauty and improving my self-worth.

Personalized Affirmation:

_____

_____

_____

_____

32. Emotional Eating and Substance Use

"The key thing is figuring out what your issues are, and it's really never about the food…I had to stop and look and ask myself, 'Why do I want this? What is the real reason?'…when you acknowledge what the issue is, you can control it better."

- Jennifer Hudson, actress and Academy Award winner

Who hasn't eaten the entire tub of ice cream, box of chocolates or drank the whole bottle? However, if it becomes a pattern, identify your triggers and manage your stress. The top performers often have excessive and compulsive traits, so know that you are at risk with your 'all or nothing' approach to life. You are smart, so can still function at work and fool everyone, but if you start an unhealthy relationship with food, alcohol or other substances, do not suffer in silence. Stop suppressing the underlying issue and seek professional help.

Example Affirmation: I am in control of my emotions and reactions.

Personalized Affirmation:

33. Obstacles

"I failed the LSAT. Basically, if I had not failed, I'd have been a lawyer and there would be no Spanx. I think failure is nothing more than life's way of nudging you that you are off course. My attitude to failure is not attached to outcome, but in not trying. It is liberating."

- Sarah Blakely, the youngest self-made female billionaire, former door-to-door fax machine salesperson and founder of Spanx

---

Ms. Blakely's father asked her daily in childhood, "So, what did you fail at today?" to emphasize that outcomes are determined by a lack of effort. Every successful person has faced adversity, but not everyone approaches hardship with the same perspective. Stretch yourself and jump those hurdles, otherwise known as obstacles.

Example Affirmation: I am overcoming obstacles by trying until I Win.

Personalized Affirmation:

_____

_____

34. Determination

"The question isn't who's going to let me; it is who is going to stop me."

- Ayn Rand, philosopher and novelist

When all else fails, ask for forgiveness, not permission. You were born to Win, so stay focused and pursue your vision. You do not need permission to step into the arena.

Example Affirmation: I am unstoppable!

Personalized Affirmation:

_____

_____

_____

_____

_____

_____

_____

_____

35. Expectations

"I have learned that as long as I hold fast to my beliefs and values - and follow my own moral compass - then the only expectations I need to live up to are my own."

— Michelle Obama, former First Lady of the United States

At some point, you have fretted over standardized tests or specialty boards. There are many "tests" as you ascend in your career. Sometimes, "the test" is deciding which job or work setting is right for you. Choosing a seemingly lucrative opportunity versus one that just feels right in your heart. Thankfully, none of these tests define you. Make the best decision you can and move forward.

Example Affirmation: I am choosing wisely when facing any test.

Personalized Affirmation:

_____

_____

_____

36. Parenthood

"I have had eight or nine miscarriages...For three years, my body has been a prisoner of trying to get pregnant—I've either been about to go into an IVF cycle, in the middle of an IVF cycle, or coming out of an IVF cycle."

- Gabrielle Union, actress and author

How can you have the family you envisioned and still meet the demands of your career? You sacrificed for years, took out loans and hoped "Mr. or Mrs. On-Point" would show up by the time you got the dream job, portfolio or C-Suite. People with prolonged training or rigorous careers often experience angst regarding the timing for parenthood. With so many options, such as adoption, single parenthood, fertility specialists, surrogacy and cryopreservation, the sky is the limit!

Example Affirmation: I can be a parent on my terms and still have an amazing career.

Personalized Affirmation:

_____

37. Take Control

"If you don't like something, change it. If you can't change it, change your attitude."

- Maya Angelou, poet and activist

Focus on what you can control. No complaining when it comes to: the weather, what other people did or did not do, your supervisor, the medical board or the corporate machine. What you can control 100 percent is your attitude about the world and circumstances that surround it. Get your mind wrapped around having a positive, proactive approach.

Example Affirmation: I am focusing on what I can control and keeping a positive attitude.

Personalized Affirmation:

_____

_____

_____

_____

38. Be the Change You Seek

"Change will not come if we wait for some other person or some other time. We are the ones we've been waiting for. We are the change that we seek."

- Barack Obama, former president of the United States

Stop just pointing out the flaws in the system. Instead of complaining and analyzing, inspire others to contribute to a solution. You are capable of more than you imagine. Your unique perspective makes you the right person to represent. Stop looking for someone else to step up and fix it. Be your own hero.

Example Affirmation: I am setting the example and capable of affecting change.

Personalized Affirmation:

_____

_____

_____

_____

39. Passion

"When you have passion for something, you tend not only to be better at it, but you work harder at it too."
-Vera Wang, fashion designer

Getting ahead requires hard work, passion and consistency. Visualize the finish line and the people you will see when you get there. It is bigger than dreaming. It is a manifestation exercise. Knowing exactly why you are working so hard is how you dig deep enough to find a way to your personal horizon against all odds.

Example Affirmation: I am visualizing my destination as I work on my passion.

Personalized Affirmation:

_____

_____

_____

_____

_____

_____

40. Dreams

"When you want something, all the universe conspires in helping you to achieve it."

- **Paulo Coehlo, novelist and author of The Alchemist.**

Do you dare to dream? Do you desire freedom, love, living abroad, wealth, power or fame? Do not worry about how you will achieve it. Speak it into existence and attract what you want. Focus on what the dream will do to improve the lives of others because altruism is a Win-Win situation.

Example Affirmation: I am dreaming bigger to improve more lives.

Personalized Affirmation:

_____

_____

_____

_____

_____

41. Failure

"It is impossible to live without failing at something, unless you live so cautiously that you might as well not have lived at all, in which case you have failed by default."

- J. K. Rowling, author of Harry Potter series, single parent and domestic violence survivor

---

Winners are not afraid of losing and would rather have a fantastic adventure while exploring something new than accept the status quo. Perceived risk may keep you from reaching all your dreams. Your 'messy' story, adversity or trials are what make you unique and could be the fodder for your ascension. Look at all the reality TV stars for more proof. If you thought you could not fail, what would you do, try or risk?

Example Affirmation: I am winning by taking risks and embracing my mess.

Personalized Affirmation:

_____

_____

_____

42. Setbacks

"Success is going from failure to failure without loss of enthusiasm."

- **Winston Churchill, army officer and British statesman**

Do not be discouraged when you face setbacks. Strength is built through adversity. No muscles are formed without resistance. No matter how many times you are knocked down, rise again.

Example Affirmation: I am growing through failure and facing each day with enthusiasm.

Personalized Affirmation:

_____

_____

_____

_____

_____

_____

Toni A. Haley, MD

43. Imposter Syndrome

"We must have perseverance and above all have confidence in ourselves. We must believe that we are gifted for something and that this thing must be attained."

- Marie Curie, physicist and chemist

Still feel like a "fraud" despite all your diplomas and awards? Do you wonder when they will figure out that you are not as smart and capable as your resume suggests? You have accomplished a lot and it's time to believe in your value. Bring your gifts, energy, and passion to the table. You will instill confidence in your abilities, even if you have to fake it 'til you make it!

Example Affirmation: I am growing my confidence and sharing my gifts.

Personalized Affirmation:

_____

_____

_____

_____

44. Choices

"I don't harp on the negative because if you do, there's no progression. There's no forward movement. You got to always look on the bright side of things, and we are in control…you have control over the choices you make."

- Taraji P. Henson, actress

You may be hurt or discouraged, but you never have to play the role of a victim. New experiences help shape you, but do not define you. Blaming others is a waste of time. If you want to improve your life or circumstance, it's a series of choices. Never have a heart of jealousy because if you want something, you can always choose to Win big.

Example Affirmation: I am reshaping my reality by making wiser choices.

Personalized Affirmation:

_____

_____

_____

_____

45. Preparation

"Be so good they can't ignore you."

- Steve Martin, actor and author

Talent does not mean that discipline is not required. Take the time to study, read and practice. Put in effort behind the scenes like an understudy waiting in the wings for an opportunity to shine. Your day is coming, so prepare.

Example Affirmation: I will prepare each day for new opportunities .

Personalized Affirmation:

_____

_____

_____

_____

_____

_____

46. Mistakes

"The only real mistake is the one from which we learn nothing."

- **Henry Ford, founder of the Ford Motor Company**

As long as you live and breathe, you will make mistakes. Congratulations! It is a sign that you have stepped out of your comfort zone. Think carefully when faced with a tough decision, but do not linger or beat yourself up. Learn, grow, and move forward.

Example Affirmation: I am forgiving past mistakes and I am always learning.

Personalized Affirmation:

_____

_____

_____

_____

_____

_____

47. Freedom

"Most people do not really want freedom because freedom involves responsibility, and most people are frightened of responsibility."

- Sigmund Freud, neurologist and founder of psychoanalysis

You want your own business, medical practice, a promotion, more money, a better schedule, bigger home, more kids? You are going to have to take on more responsibility. Say yes to the freedom of choice and step up to the plate.

Example Affirmation: I am embracing the freedom to choose and take full responsibility.

Personalized Affirmation:

_____

_____

_____

_____

_____

48. Dating

"If he invited you out, he's got to pay."

- Beyoncé Knowles, singer and actress

High performing ladies *love* to be in control. Yes, you are an independent woman and you can take yourself out to dinner, but he invited you. Let's see what he wants to show you, shall we? Chivalry is not dead, unless you stab it repeatedly with your credit card. Some things can be old-school. Winners, know when to step back and allow a man to court you. It does not diminish your power.

Example Affirmation: I am allowing others to take the lead and accept their generosity.

Personalized Affirmation:

_____

_____

_____

_____

_____

49. Discrimination

"Sometimes I feel discriminated against but it does not make me angry. It merely astonishes me. How can any deny themselves the pleasure of my company? It's beyond me."

- Zora Neale Hurston, novelist, folklorist and author of Their Eyes Were Watching God

---

Remain confident in your abilities, your value and your expertise. Others may oppose you, overlook you or snub you. Chalk it up to their fear that *your excellence diminishes their shine.* Do not waste emotions or time worrying over their limited experiences. Show up and Win!

Example Affirmation: I am shining and Winning despite the bias of others.

Personalized Affirmation:

_____

_____

_____

50. Vision and Affirmations

"I say something, and then it usually happens. Maybe not on schedule, but it usually happens." -

> Elon Musk, billionaire, innovator, CEO and co-founder of Tesla

You can bring anything to fruition once you can fathom it and speak it. You do not owe anyone an explanation or justification. Your vision is *not defined by your education, career, or upbringing*. When you glimpse at your future, it should ignite your passion for innovation. Speak it out into the atmosphere until it happens.

Example Affirmation: I am speaking my truth and taking action to Win.

Personalized Affirmation:

_____

_____

_____

_____

51. Sexism

"We as men have been incredibly ignorant about what's happening right underneath our noses. The women who are now sharing their painful experience are some of the richest, most powerful, and beloved women in the country. And if they are fearful of speaking out, just imagine how hard it must be for every other woman in the world."

— Jim Jeffries, actor, writer and comedian.

It takes a village of *men and women* who agree to support and advocate for talent, regardless of gender. From surgeons to world leaders to CEOs, we have proven that both sexes are capable and worthy of respect. Women, let's lift one another up and educate and enlist men to advocate for us. Men, help women get equal pay for equal work and experience. While we are at it, let's get rid of all the *–isms*: racism, classism, sexism.

Example Affirmation: I am helping other women advance as I climb.

Personalized Affirmation:

52. #MeToo

"I want all the girls watching to know a new day is on the horizon…And when that new day finally dawns, it will be because of a lot of magnificent women…and some pretty phenomenal men, fighting hard to make sure they are the leaders to take us to the time where nobody has to say 'me too' again."

- **Oprah Winfrey, in her acceptance speech as the first female African American recipient of the Cecile B. DeMille Award for outstanding contributions to the world of entertainment**

Tarana Burke's original movement, which started in 2006, inspired the #MeToo hashtag. It originally was intended to empower young women of color who were victims of sexual abuse, assault or exploitation to identify each other to facilitate healing. Through empathy, they can combat feelings of shame, isolation and powerlessness.

Example Affirmation: My feelings are valid and I remain powerful.

Personalized Affirmation:

53. Patience

"As a younger person, my philosophy was jump off a cliff. I realize now that there are stairs and elevators. I am learning every day to allow the space between where I am and where I want to be to inspire me and not terrify me. I can even ask for help! Not feeling that I have to know everything, and that's where the growth comes in, in the not knowing."

— **Tracee Ellis Ross, actress, model, comedian and television host**

Remember when you were looking at your vision board every day? You were applying for your dream school, sending resumes to the top company, trying to make the Dean's List, imagining the places you would travel, pledging your sorority or fraternity and still trying to enjoy the moment. Winners, you have reasons to celebrate your achievements *right now*, so reevaluate your perspective and count your blessings.

Example Affirmation: I am embracing the moment.

Personalized Affirmation:

---

54. Entrepreneurship

"Entrepreneurs have a great ability to create change, be flexible, build companies and cultivate the kind of work environment in which they want to work."

- Tory Burch, CEO, designer and founder of the Tory Burch Foundation

---

"Dream job" got you down? Tired of working hard on someone else's dream with no fulfillment, crabby co-workers and long hours? Start by having a seat at the table to learn and grow, but please build your own table. Long hours are usually required either way, so why not create *your vision*? More time with your loved ones, travel and freedom to make your own rules is reason enough to build your own company.

Example Affirmation: I am capable of building a company where I enjoy working.

Personalized Affirmation:

_____

_____

_____

55. Giving Back

"If you want to lift yourself up, lift up someone else."
- Booker T. Washington, leader, educator and author

You have an abundant life, so you have a responsibility to others. You may share your gifts with friends and family, then expand your giving to include the larger community. There is work to be done both domestically and abroad. Your vision should be big enough for a lasting legacy that benefits multiple generations. All you give will multiply tenfold, so be generous.

Example Affirmation: By lifting others, I am lifting myself higher.

Personalized Affirmation:

_____

_____

_____

_____

_____

56. Stress

"I felt in a lot of instances I was deliberately being put through stress because when you're a guy who generates money, people have a vested interest in controlling you."

- Dave Chappelle, comedian, actor and author

Micromanagement and administrative duties are a source of stress for many high performers. A 2013 Towers Watson survey cited work-related stress as the number one occupational hazard. Managing your energy, exercising, laughter, social support and taking 20-minute breaks are stress management techniques recommended by the American Psychological Association.

Example Affirmation: I am in control of how much stress I experience.

Personalized Affirmation:

_____

_____

_____

_____

57. Sleep

"Sleep is the best meditation."

- **Dalai Lama, spiritual leader**

According to the Centers for Disease Control and Prevention (CDC), inadequate sleep leads to worker error, low productivity and safety hazards. Have you ever sacrificed sleep for a presentation, concert or exam? This trend may continue or even worsen depending on your chosen career path. Consider making changes if your schedule is not sustainable.

Example Affirmation: I will sleep to prevent errors and improve productivity.

Personalized Affirmation:

_____

_____

_____

_____

_____

Toni A. Haley, MD

58. Boundaries

"Boy, Bye!"

— Angela Rye, political commentator, attorney and CEO of Impact Strategies

---

How many times has someone with a fraction of your education tried to dictate your workflow or vacation request? How about those family members who expect you to bail them out of every bad decision? Winners, it is *your* responsibility to teach people how to treat you! You do not have to accept abuse or disrespect.

Example Affirmation: I teach people how to treat me by establishing boundaries.

Personalized Affirmation:

_____

_____

_____

_____

_____

59. Self-Esteem

"No one can make you feel inferior without your consent."

- Eleanor Roosevelt, former First Lady of the United States and activist

The rigors of training or building a career, especially in a toxic environment, can have lasting effects. You may begin to question your ability or self-worth. Ask others where your strengths lie, accept compliments graciously and get to work excelling in those areas. Seeing consistent evidence of your skills can lead to improved self-image and quality relationships.

Example Affirmation: I am a smart doctor!

Personalized Affirmation:

_____

_____

_____

_____

_____

60. Legacy

"If your dream only includes you, it's too small."
— Ava DuVernay, director, writer and producer

Winners make their mark on the world! You can pass down property, money or other material items, but you also can also pass on lessons learned to your loved ones or students you mentor. Who will you contribute to in your lifetime?

Example Affirmation: I am building a Winning legacy to add value in my community!

Personalized Affirmation:

_____

_____

_____

_____

_____

_____

61. Loneliness

"You have to stand for what you believe in and sometimes you have to stand alone."

- Queen Latifah, actress and rapper

You are busy creating the life you want and do not have time to explain your actions. Surround yourself with people who understand, but be prepared to go solo. Seeking validation or company on the journey can take you off your path. Most innovators don't have buy-in on their ideas until they are already successful. Not everyone will be on board with your decisions, and that is okay.

Example Affirmation: I am willing to pursue my dreams alone.

Personalized Affirmation:

_____

_____

_____

_____

62. Faith

"Faith is taking the first step even when you don't see the whole staircase."

- Martin Luther King Jr., civil rights leader, activist and minister

When your resolve starts to wax and wane, think of all the reasons you started on this journey at the outset and keep going. Winners rest, regroup or reroute, but never quit.

Example Affirmation: I am faithful and will finish what I start.

Personalized Affirmation:

_____

_____

_____

_____

_____

_____

63. Mental Health

"Women in particular need to keep an eye on their physical and mental health, because if we're scurrying to and from appointments and errands, we don't have a lot of time to take care of ourselves."

- Michelle Obama, former First Lady of the United States

News flash: you are human. Take the same advice you give others. Schedule regular doctor appointments, vacations, and spa days, attend church, hire a therapist and engage in recreation. Employee assistance programs at work may offer confidential mental health services. Do not wait for a crisis to address your mental health.

Example Affirmation: I am Winning when I prioritize my mental health!

Personalized Affirmation:

_____

_____

_____

64. Losing

"The reality is: sometimes you lose. And you're never too good to lose. You're never too big to lose. You're never too smart to lose. It happens."

- Beyoncé Knowles, singer and actress

On the road to the top, sometimes you Win, sometimes you fall flat on your face and get a concussion. The treatment for traumatic brain injury, is rest. When you make a misstep, take a step back and regroup. You have everything you need to pick up the pieces and try again.

Example Affirmation: Losing does not define me or keep me down.

Personalized Affirmation:

_____

_____

_____

_____

_____

Toni A. Haley, MD

65. Worry

"If you can't sleep, get up and do something instead of lying there worrying. It's the worry that gets you, not the lack of sleep."

- Dale Carnegie, writer and leadership trainer

Your mind will not rest easily when your spirit is unsettled. Sleep hygiene or a bedtime routine is the best way to prevent restlessness and insomnia. For interrupted sleep, try reading, meditation, exercise or *even sex* to get back to sleep. Doctor's orders!

Example Affirmation: I am releasing worry and focusing on what I can control.

Personalized Affirmation:

_____

_____

_____

_____

_____

66. Love

"When you get to a place where you understand that love and belonging, your worthiness, is a birthright and not something you have to earn, anything is possible."

- Brené Brown, author and research professor

Children should not have to earn the love of their parents because it is their birthright. Everyone is worthy from birth, so open your heart to receive it. The "default setting" should be love and acceptance in your relationships.

Example Affirmation: I am worthy of love and belonging.

Personalized Affirmation:

_____

_____

_____

_____

_____

67. Death and Letting Go

"I think when tragedy occurs it presents a choice. You can give in to the void: the emptiness that fills your heart, your lungs, constricts your ability to think or even breathe. Or you can try to find meaning."

- **Sheryl Sandberg, COO of Facebook, author and founder of Leanin.org**

Patients die in spite of all that the medical team did without any error. Patients live in spite of fallible human doctor errors. In the grand scheme of things, you can only do your best. It is not wholly up to you who lives or dies on any given day.

Example Affirmation: I am Winning by letting go of what is not under my control.

Personalized Affirmation:

_____

_____

_____

_____

68. Vulnerability

"Through my research, I found that vulnerability is the glue that holds relationships together... vulnerability is the birthplace of connection and the path to the feeling of worthiness."

- Brené Brown, author and research professor

Open up and share your story of adversity or Winning against the odds. The world is drawn to you when you have an air of confidence and embrace your story. Get off the sidelines and live authentically!

Example Affirmation: Being vulnerable helps me connect with other Winners.

Personalized Affirmation:

_____

_____

_____

_____

_____

69. Comparison

"I generally find that comparison is the fast track to unhappiness. No one ever compares themselves to someone and comes out even. Nine times out of ten, we compare ourselves to people somehow better than us and end up feeling more inadequate."

- Jack Canfield, corporate trainer and bestselling coauthor of Chicken Soup for the Soul series

---

Remember that teacher who said, "Keep your eyes on your own paper"? Winners, focus on your goals and plans, and visualize where you are going. Don't trip over your own feet while looking elsewhere and getting distracted. Social media has made it more common for people to feel that they do not measure up, but no one shows you what is going on behind the scenes.

Example Affirmation: I am living according to my personal standard of excellence.

Personalized Affirmation:

_____

_____

70. Debt

"Recast your current problems into proactive goals."
- Suze Orman, author, financial advisor and motivational speaker

How much you earn does not matter if you keep very little or blow the budget. Student loans, cars, medical bills, internships, family obligations or home ownership are reasons high performers accumulate debt. You need a comprehensive strategy to determine the best use of your resources. You deserve nice things, but what are you doing to reign in expenses, plan for retirement, protect your assets/estate and pay lower interest rates? Winners, take action to address your finances and write time-sensitive goals.

Example Affirmation: I am taking a proactive approach to debt and finances and writing down my goals.

Personalized Affirmation:

_____

_____

_____

71. Mentorship

"Tell me and I forget, teach me and I may remember, involve me and I learn."

- **Benjamin Franklin, founding father of the United States**

See one, do one, teach one…that was how our professors nudged us to gain experience and get hands-on practice in medicine. It is easy to criticize the youth, but are you willing to show them the way and groom them to lead after you retire?

Example Affirmation: I am mentoring the next generation to Win.

Personalized Affirmation:

_____

_____

_____

_____

_____

72. Networking

"There's a fast track if you can do the networking. For some personalities it works, but for mine it doesn't."

- Idris Elba, actor

Outgoing, shy, introvert, extrovert…not everyone is comfortable with networking. Stop hiding out and avoiding work functions and social gatherings. If you are invited, attend various events, so you know what is going on in your department, company, hospital system, network or community. Resist the urge to disconnect from your colleagues.

Example Affirmation: I will begin networking to make connections.

Personalized Affirmation:

_____

_____

_____

_____

_____

73. Intuition

"Intuition will tell the thinking mind where to look next."

- Jonas Salk, medical researcher and virologist

Although you are a logical thinker and have umpteen years of education, you also have a powerful intuition. You cannot always put your finger on it, but it guides you. Listen to your inner voice because some of the best experiences are based on the intangible.

Example Affirmation: I am trusting my intuition.

Personalized Affirmation:

_____

_____

_____

_____

_____

_____

_____

74. Excuses

"Ninety-nine percent of the failures come from people who have the habit of making excuses."

- George Washington Carver, inventor, botanist and scientist

All that time you spent creating an excuse, you could have completed the task. Do the hard things *first* so procrastination, dread or frustration do not take over. Carpe diem!

Example Affirmation: I am eliminating excuses.

Personalized Affirmation:

_____

_____

_____

_____

_____

_____

75. Fancy Titles

"Organization charts and fancy titles count for next to nothing."

- Colin Powell, American elder statesman, former national security advisor and commander of the US Army

---

We all know people with titles or a designated parking space. Do you have authority? Autonomy? Is the additional responsibility compensated fairly? Are the perks getting you closer to your personal goals, or is it just a title and a lot more meetings?

Example Affirmation: I am deserving of more than a just a title.

Personalized Affirmation:

_____

_____

_____

_____

_____

76. Awe

"Go outside and turn your attention to the many miracles around you. This five-minute-a-day regimen of appreciation and gratitude will help you to focus your life in awe."

- Dr. Wayne Dyer, philosopher, motivational speaker and author of Your Erroneous Zones

---

Researchers at University of California and NYU found that people who experience a sense of awe have better mental health. They felt more purposeful, social, altruistic and connected. Connect with nature and tap into your sense of wonder. Experience things the way you did as a child with spontaneity and excitement.

Example Affirmation: I am appreciating the world around me with gratitude.

Personalized Affirmation:

_____

_____

_____

_____

77. Meditation

"The more man meditates upon good thoughts, the better will be his world and the world at large."

— Confucius, philosopher and founder of Confucianism

Starting each day with a routine, a clear mind, improved focus, better immunity, reduced stress, happiness and self-awareness sounds like a plan! Meditation is linked to all of the above. Winners make time for meditation each day.

Example Affirmation: Relaxing my mind and body is rejuvenating.

Personalized Affirmation:

_____

_____

_____

_____

_____

78. Sponsorship

"The best way a mentor can prepare another leader is to expose him or her to other great people."

–John C. Maxwell, Author and Business Trainer

If you've made it this far, you've had your share of mentors. One thing you can do above teaching is to expose mentees to people who can help further their career. Allow mentees to expand their network through you and watch your legacy grow!

Example Affirmation: I am committed to introducing mentees to Winners.

Personalized Affirmation:

_____

_____

_____

_____

_____

_____

79. Job Fit

"If you don't feel it, flee from it. Go where you are celebrated, not merely tolerated."

- Paul F. Davis, author, motivational speaker and life coach

You will never reach your true potential if the job fit is wrong. Your values, experiences, workplace culture, recognition, collegiality and challenges all determine if an opportunity is right for you. Do you feel out of place and undervalued, or are your contributions downplayed? It may be time to move on or build something of your own. Be very deliberate about where you work, who you spend your time with and how you allocate your time. Your resume will have more continuity and you will be more productive, happy and inspired.

Example Affirmation: I am deliberate in choosing where I fit.

Personalized Affirmation:

_____

_____

80. Criticism

"I like constructive criticism from smart people."
   - Prince, legendary writer, singer and performer

All criticism is not constructive and you need to be wary of the source. It is okay to care what people think as long as they are people you admire, trust and respect. Do not be offended when someone offers guidance. Winners grow from positive feedback.

Example Affirmation: I welcome constructive criticism.

Personalized Affirmation:

_____

_____

_____

_____

_____

_____

81. Regret

"We must all suffer one of two things: the pain of discipline or the pain of regret or disappointment."

- Jim Rohn, entrepreneur, author and motivational speaker

The pain of regret or disappointment is usually present when you made a decision based on fear or short-term comfort. Set your sights on something you choose to pursue and be disciplined in working towards accomplishing the goal. Winners make sacrifices to experience the freedom of choice.

Example Affirmation: I choose to be disciplined and face my fears.

Personalized Affirmation:

_____

_____

_____

_____

82. Motivation

"People often say that motivation doesn't last. Well, neither does bathing - that's why we recommend it daily."

- Zig Ziglar, motivational speaker and author

Set your intentions *every single day*. Listen to your favorite motivational speech, read motivational quotes and scriptures. Surround yourself with Winning words and examples.

Example Affirmation: I start each day with affirmations, motivational words and intentions.

Personalized Affirmation:

_____

_____

_____

_____

_____

_____

83. Rules

"You don't learn to walk by following the rules. You learn by doing, and by falling over."

- Sir Richard Branson, business mogul and philanthropist

You tend to follow the rules. Most of the time it works out. For the rare instances when you step outside of the box, be bold and make a new path. Winners transcend rules to lead and innovate.

Example Affirmation: I am boldly breaking the rules and stepping outside the box.

Personalized Affirmation:

_____

_____

_____

_____

_____

_____

84. Decisions

"It's not hard to make decisions when you know what your values are."

> **- Roy E. Disney, senior executive for the Walt Disney Company**

Stay on the moral high ground and do not lower your standards. Know what you value because Winners are not afraid to walk away from opportunities or people who lack substance. Stick to your values and treat them like a Winner's playbook.

Example Affirmation: I am making solid decisions based on my values.

Personalized Affirmation:

_____

_____

_____

_____

_____

85. Guilt

"Every man is guilty of all the good he did not do."
   - **Voltaire, philosopher and enlightenment writer**

Good intentions do not count, so guilt has an upside. It compels you to take action and make a way, not an excuse. We are all busy, but make time for the people and the causes that are dear to your heart. Regret and missed opportunities will cause more heartache than giving freely.

Example Affirmation: I am releasing guilt and making room for what matters to me.

Personalized Affirmation:

_____

_____

_____

_____

_____

_____

86. Authenticity

"I had no idea that being your authentic self could make me as rich as I've become. If I had, I'd have done it a lot earlier."

- Oprah Winfrey, media icon and philanthropist

Taboo topics that were once shrouded in secrecy are now shared to connect with others and build communities. Winners embrace their truth and compel others to step into the light. Your deepest hurt or secret is likely the key to emotional and financial freedom.

Example Affirmation: My authentic self is the key to my health and wealth.

Personalized Affirmation:

_____

_____

_____

_____

_____

87. Effort

"As much as talent counts, effort counts twice."

- Angela Duckworth, author and founder and CEO of Character Lab

---

Show up early. Stay late. Stay prepared. Rest. Repeat. You don't have to know everything, but be willing to work harder than you did yesterday as you build your future. Residency or getting "the job" was just the warm up, so roll up your sleeves and get to work.

Example Affirmation: I will put in the effort it takes to win.

Personalized Affirmation:

_____

_____

_____

_____

_____

_____

88. Resilience

"Always remember, you have within you the strength, the patience, and the passion to reach for the stars to change the world."

- **Harriet Tubman, abolitionist and humanitarian**

Got GRIT (Goal-Directed Resilience in Training)? A 2015 study by Angela Duckworth demonstrated how resilience is the main reason high achievers Win. *Grit is as essential as intelligence.* Your ancestors fought and perished for you to have more opportunities. The Montgomery, Alabama Bus Boycott lasted 381 days to protest segregation on public transportation. Winning requires you to stay the course through trauma or hardship and inspire others to Win too!

Example Affirmation: I am becoming more resilient despite adversity.

Personalized Affirmation:

_____

_____

_____

89. Work-Life Integration

"Integrate what you believe in every single area of your life. Take your heart to work and ask the most and best of everybody else, too."

- Meryl Streep, award-winning actress and philanthropist

High performers and achievers who seek the perfect balance are in for a rude awakening. Between career, parenthood, marriage, aging parents and maintaining friendships, each day has a new twist. The best approach? *Do what you love with people who share your values.* It is a Win-Win situation that keeps you grounded and supported as you strive for more.

Example Affirmation: I am integrating my values in every area of my life.

Personalized Affirmation:

_____

_____

_____

_____

90. Gratitude

"Thank you is the best prayer that anyone can say. I say that one a lot. Thank you expresses extreme gratitude, humility, understanding."

- **Alice Walker, novelist, political activist and author of The Color Purple**

When you are grateful for what you already have, more comes your way. A daily gratitude practice can improve your career, health, personality, relationships and lead to more joy. Winners, you have several reasons to express gratitude every day!

Example Affirmation: I give thanks for health, prosperity, and limitless potential!

Personalized Affirmation:

_____

_____

_____

_____

_____

91. Delegate and Reclaim Your Time

"Productivity is never an accident. It is always the result of a commitment to excellence, intelligent planning, and focused effort."

- Paul J. Meyer, Leadership Management Institute founder

Winners—prioritize, allow nothing to interrupt your flow and learn the art of delegation! You have increased productivity when you work for less than an hour and take breaks. You need protected time with no interruptions. Never perform a task you can hire someone else to do below your hourly rate. It will save you "bandwidth" to think and create in your areas of expertise or passion. Stop being *busy* and do what is *urgent*. Ask yourself every hour, "What is the most valuable use of my time and which task is in line with my goals right now?"

Example Affirmation: I am my best when I prioritize, take breaks and delegate.

Personalized Affirmation:

_____

_____

92. Live in the Moment

"There are only two days in the year that nothing can be done. One is called yesterday and the other is called tomorrow, so today is the right day to love, believe, do and mostly live."

- Dalai Lama, spiritual leader

You are distracted. A lot. I know you are important and everything, with all your fancy titles and multiple cell phones. However, do you remember why you started? What is the foundation for all of this busyness? So you mean to tell me, you don't have time for a quick call to your friend? You need to be fully present when you make plans to be with your loved ones. Your faith and relationships are the foundation for all of your hard work. So live in the moment to embrace the life you always envisioned.

Example Affirmation: I am committing to be present in the moment.

Personalized Affirmation:

_____

_____

93. Leader versus Manager

"Management is efficiency in climbing the ladder of success; leadership determines whether the ladder is leaning against the right wall."

- Dr. Stephen R. Covey, educator, speaker and author of *The 7 Habits of Highly Effective People*

Are you a manager or a leader? Are you a task driver, or an innovator? Step away from your desk and get involved in the project or operation on all levels at intervals. Assess if things are working the way you imagined in all of those long planning meetings. You will earn respect if you take responsibility for outcomes and develop your team based on their interests and skill sets. Applaud innovation in those around you and inspire others to think creatively.

Example Affirmation: I am leading instead of merely managing.

Personalized Affirmation:

_____

_____

94. Lifelong Learning

"And in order to succeed in later life, you need creative skills because look at how fast the world is changing."

- Robert Sternberg, professor of human development at Cornell University and former president of the University of Wyoming

---

Change is inevitable, so if you want to remain contemporary, you must grow. *Daily*. Implement lifelong learning incrementally, no matter your position or job title. Commit to trade magazines, blogs, podcasts and books, and through networking and conferences. You must continually learn and grow. Most millionaires and billionaires read as a pastime for education over entertainment.

Example Affirmation: I am a lifelong learner who reads and improves my skill set.

Personalized Affirmation:

_____

_____

_____

95. Motivating Others

"Outstanding leaders go out of their way to boost the self-esteem of their personnel. If people believe in themselves, it's amazing what they can accomplish."

Sam Walton, founder of Wal-Mart and Sam's Club

How often do you give your staff or colleagues positive feedback on a specific area where they really shine? You can motivate your team by simply acknowledging and praising positive attributes and contributions. Increased confidence will lead to increased competence and accomplishments.

Example Affirmation: I am building my team's self-esteem.

Personalized Affirmation:

_____

_____

_____

_____

_____

Toni A. Haley, MD

96. Conflict

"I have sadness in me. I have anger in me. I have heartbreak in me."

- Ellen DeGeneres, talk show host, comedian, and one of the world's highest-paid celebrities according to *Forbes Magazine*

Ever 'blow up' or cry for no apparent reason? Frustrated with trying to keep the peace and haven't expressed your true thoughts? Winners and high performers can still be hurt, heartbroken, mistreated, angry or resentful. When you avoid confronting those feelings or hold onto unresolved issues, those feelings can grow. Communication is the key to feeling more empowered. Avoid shutting down or isolating yourself. Address concerns in a straightforward manner and you will be surprised how relieved you are when it is no longer weighing you down.

Example Affirmation: I am expressing myself to prevent conflict.

Personalized Affirmation:

97. Micromanaging

"The best leader is the one who has sense enough to pick good men to do what he wants done, and the self-restraint to keep from meddling with them while they do it."

— Theodore Roosevelt, former president of the United States

Micromanage much? Remember the supervisor who watched over your shoulder and criticized every move before you had a chance to think it through? Do you miss that one? No. Do you want others to feel that way? Not really. Choose your team, then let them execute the plan. You trust your judgment, right?

Example Affirmation: I choose staff that can do the job.

Personalized Affirmation:

_____

_____

_____

_____

_____

98. Try Until You Win

"Women have to harness their power—it's absolutely true. It's just learning not to take the first no. And if you can't go straight ahead, you go around the corner."

- Cher, legendary singer, actress and philanthropist

'No' really means 'next opportunity.' Whether it's applying for residency, seeking a promotion, or trying on bathing suits, it may take more than one try to get it right. There's more than one way to get something done, and companies are hiring people from diverse backgrounds to lead now more than ever. *If they tell you no, consider it practice.* Know your value and find another door or institution that recognizes your value.

Example Affirmation: I am becoming more confident in seeking new opportunities.

Personalized Affirmation:

_____

_____

_____

_____

99. Character

"Leadership is a potent combination of strategy and character. But if you must be without one, be without the strategy"

- Herbert Norman Schwarzkopf, US Army General and Gulf War Veteran

---

You will not always know the answer. Be honest and transparent and willing to ask for help or consult with those who specialize in your area of weakness. People respect your leadership qualities not just your knowledge and abilities. You don't have to know everything to lead, but you do have to have strong character if you expect people to follow.

Example Affirmation: My character is the foundation for my leadership.

Personalized Affirmation:

_____

_____

_____

_____

100. Best-Laid Plans

"The heart of man plans his way, but the Lord establishes his steps."

- Proverbs 16:9

Our best-laid plans often go awry and we may not immediately know what is best in the long run. Always *create a contingency plan* and know the location of all 'emergency exits'. Believing in your mission or vision is often enough to get started on the path. Failure is not final, especially if you are proactive and have faith.

Example Affirmation: I am making plans but I am open to change.

Personalized Affirmation:

_____

_____

_____

_____

_____

Toni A. Haley, MD

Final Thoughts

"Why waste time proving over and over how great you are, when you could be getting better? Why hide deficiencies instead of overcoming them?...The passion for stretching yourself and sticking to it...is the hallmark of the growth mindset. This is the mindset that allows people to thrive during some of the most challenging times in their lives."

> ~ Carol Dweck, PhD, world-renowned Stanford University psychologist and leading authority on Mindset

High performers, you have chased success for so long, it is time to grow in a new way. Inspiration and affirmations will help you only if you use them daily, consistently and with conviction. Here are things to keep in mind, so you can Win with affirmations and reprogram your mindset.

What are your favorite quotes and affirmations? List the pages here for easy reference.

_____

_____

_____

Where are you posting your favorite affirmations so you see them every day and speak them out loud?

_____

_____

_____

What time of day will you repeat your affirmations (morning, afternoon and night)?

_____

_____

_____

Who will you share this book with?

_____

_____

_____

Now that you have so many inspirational quotes and affirmations, are you ready to take *action*? Be sure to join the VIP community of Winners to take charge of your life and surround yourself with other high performers and "VIPs" who are working on their game plan!

**Join the Winners Circle:
www.DrToniMDVIP.com**

About the Author

Dr. Toni A. Haley is a nationally recognized board-certified family medicine physician, wife, and lifestyle coach. Dr. Toni is passionate about empowering physicians and high performers to take control of their holistic health, careers, and relationships to create the life of their dreams and build enduring legacies. Her physician clients say she is "just what the doctor ordered" because she uses her authentic voice and personal story of recovery from failure by mastering her mindset. Dr. Toni earned her bachelor's degree from Morgan State University and her medical degree from Ross University, and completed her residency at Southern Illinois University.

She is happily married to Christopher R. Haley and bonus mom to two young adults. She enjoys travel, fitness and making memories.

Schedule a Free Strategy Session at
www.AskDrToniMD.com

CREATING DISTINCTIVE BOOKS WITH INTENTIONAL RESULTS

We're a collaborative group of creative masterminds with a mission to produce high-quality books to position you for monumental success in the marketplace.

Our professional team of writers, editors, designers, and marketing strategists work closely together to ensure that every detail of your book is a clear representation of the message in your writing.

Want to know more?
Write to us at info@publishyourgift.com
or call (888) 949-6228

Discover great books, exclusive offers, and more at
www.PublishYourGift.com

Connect with us on social media

@publishyourgift

www.ingramcontent.com/pod-product-compliance
Lightning Source LLC
Chambersburg PA
CBHW071608080526
44588CB00010B/1056